The Author

Derek Walters is one of the few practising specialists of
Chinese Astrology in the Western hemisphere.

Born in the Year of the Fire-Rat, during the Wood-season,
in a Dragon-month, he takes his opportunism from the
Rat, the Wood accounts for his creative side, and the Fire,
a scientific leaning; while the influence of the Dragon is
the stimulus for his interest in astrology.

Text Copyright © Derek Walters 1988

Compilation Copyright © Pagoda Books 1988

Illustrations: Endpapers, from a Chinese horoscope calendar for
the year 877, courtesy The British Library; p.17, from a Ming Encyclopedia,
dated 1610; page 29, the character for happiness; and page 33, the three
symbols for happiness, dignities and longevity from Researches into
Chinese Superstitions by H. Doré, Shanghai, 1917.

ISBN 0946326 67 3

Printed in Great Britain by
Purnell Book Production Limited

Cast Your Chinese Horoscope

THE ROOSTER

D E R E K   W A L T E R S

Contents

Introduction

*O*ur Destiny! Are we the rulers of our Fate? Are our lives shaped merely by chance circumstances? Or is the future already mapped out for us?

Few people, whatever their beliefs, could honestly say that future events hold little interest for them. Millions of readers worldwide turn to the astrological columns in their newspapers ever day; while at fairs and festivals, fortune-tellers are always sure to be a popular attraction. For the Chinese, meanwhile, a consultation with the seer at the local temple is traditionally regarded a serious matter, not to be undertaken lightly. Indeed, on any day of the week – morning, afternoon and night – Chinese temples, such as the Wong Tai Sin in Kowloon or the ancient Lung Shan in Taipei, are filled with throngs of devout worshippers, who have come to enquire from the monks what the prospects are for future happiness, security, and health.

In ancient times, astrology was a highly secret art, for it was thought that the movements of the stars were messages from the gods to the Emperor, and thus far too important for the eyes and ears of common folk. Every person at the court was represented by one of the stars in the Heavens: and the Emperor's, of course, was the Pole Star, round which, as Confucius said, 'all the other stars make obeisance.' The stars closest to the Pole Star represented the Emperor's family, while round them rotated the stars of the ministers, generals, and nobility. As they twinkled, glimmered or faded, so the fortunes of the court officials were revealed.

With the growth of the Chinese empire, its traders and merchants grew more prosperous; and although they were not important enough to have their own stars in the sky, they were sufficiently well-off to persuade the temple monks to cast their horoscopes for them. It was a crime punishable by death for anyone other than the official court astrologers to study the heavens, but the monks were clever enough to realise that the motions of the stars and planets were sufficiently regular and ordered to enable them to calculate horoscopes based solely on the day of birth. Accordingly, a new branch of astrology developed in China — *Ming Shu*, meaning literally 'the reckoning of Fate'.

In the course of time, the temple astrologer began to play a role as important as a registrar of births, marriages and deaths, and these were the occasions when he was most likely to be in demand: and today, too, Chinese temples have their forecourts and side booths where the temple astrologers can be consulted. Even in mainland China, where 'superstitious practices' are frowned upon by the authorities, orange-robed priests sit patiently in the quiet temples, deftly applying brush-stroke calligraphy to the red paper horoscopes which are still eagerly sought after by the faithful few. In Taiwan, too, old traditions are carefully maintained as a way of life. There, at the great temples, so many astrologers are busy working that their booths overflow the temple grounds into the streets and the subway below, where many of them even have their own private telephones!

According to Chinese tradition, when a child is born, an astrologer is called on to cast horoscopes, and this is usually sealed and kept in a special box throughout the child's life. Often, too, marriages will not be contracted between two families until both parties have consulted their astrologers to ensure that the couple's horoscopes show that they are a compatible pair.

On New Year's Day, Chinese families from Hong Kong to San Francisco, whether or not they are able to go to the expense of employing a professional astrologer to see what the coming year holds in store for them, will certainly buy the new yearly almanac. This is hung at home in a prominent place, where it can be consulted for daily directions and advice on almost every conceivable action, from digging trenches to washing hair. (This might seem odd to the western reader at first; but in fact the western world also has many similar customs with traditional days for doing the laundry, going to market – and even for eating fish or turkey!) The Chinese pay great attention to the almanac's instructions, not just for social convenience, but because it is believed that the penalties for ignoring such daily directions include dire punishment in the world-to-come.

The twelve animals of Chinese astrology

The ancient Chinese first began to study astrology many thousands of years ago, centuries or more before they had made contact with the West: so that by the time that a thriving trade had opened up across the vast continent of Asia, their system of astrology was already firmly established, with quite a different form from the western practice. Even the patterns of stars which shape the constellations were seen quite differently by the ancient Chinese: and the names given to the constellations are significantly different, too. Whereas in the West, many of the names of the stars and constellations have a nautical touch about them, suggesting that the stars were given their names by a people who lived near the sea or who were sea-faring, many Chinese star names, on the other hand, refer to horses and carriages, suggesting a nation that was more at home inland than on the water.

But the most noticeable difference lies at the very heart of popular astrology. In the West, when someone asks about your star-sign, he is really asking which *month* you were born in. The Chinese, however, like to know what *year* you were born in. The twelve animals of Chinese astrology – the so-called 'Chinese Zodiac' – are used to name the different years in one Great Year of twelve ordinary years. So, according to your particular year of birth, you may be a Rat, Ox, Tiger or Hare; a Dragon, Snake, Horse or Sheep; a Monkey, Rooster, Dog or Pig.

How, when, or why these animals were chosen to represent their particular years is a mystery which perplexes scholars to this day. Legend says that the Buddha summoned all the animals, and that these twelve were the only ones which answered. It is more likely, however, that these animal names were carefully chosen by ancient astrologers because they seemed to be the best ones to represent the characteristics of people born in those years, and also indicated what the events of coming years might be like.

As you become acquainted with the characteristics of each animal year, remember that the Chinese interpretation is often very different from western ideas. Some people find it far from flattering to learn that they were born in Rat or Pig years, for example: but to the Chinese, the Rat is the symbol of ingenuity; and the Pig, a sign of comfort. You can discover more about your own animal type on pages 17-20; while if you turn to the section beginning on page 21, you will find how you are likely to fare in each different animal year.

Yin and Yang signs

The twelve animal signs are conveniently grouped into six pairs – the first of each pair considered to have *yang* or active attributes, the second possessing softer *yin* qualities. Thus, the creative Rat is paired with the practical Ox; the competitive Tiger with the diplomatic Hare; the exuberant Dragon with the prudent Snake; the convivial Horse with the rather astute Rooster; and the faithful Dog with the caring Pig.

According to Chinese beliefs, all things are made from differing proportions of *yin* and *yang*. It is even sometimes said that these two forces correspond to 'female' and 'male'; but in reality, they are only terms of convenience. Thus in any one personality, *yin* and *yang* represent the opposing sides of human character, the passive and the active, the imaginative and the logical, as well as the creative and the destructive.

Personality revealed

Each pair of animal signs further combines to form one of the six aspects of destiny known to astrologers as 'Houses.' Not only do these help to paint a character portrait, they also reveal the likely trends of fortune for different periods of time – years, months, days, or hours – which are associated with each animal.

The Rat and Ox represent beginnings and completions of projects in the *House of Construction*; the Tiger and the Hare symbolise the aggressive and diplomatic paths to personal achievement in the *House of Expansion*; the Dragon and the Snake reflect the extrovert and introspective sides of personality in the *House of Mystery*; the Horse and Sheep reveal the basic differences in interests shown by both sexes in the *House of Gender*; craftsmanship and flair are the two qualities essential to success represented by the Monkey and the Rooster in the *House of Career*; and finally, the Dog, symbolising friendship and protection, and the Pig symbolising the home, its comforts, and also offspring, belong to the *House of Family*.

Many people, when they first encounter Chinese astrology, find it hard to accept the general principle that everyone born in a particular year will have the same basic characteristics. But in fact this is one of Chinese astrology's most convincing factors: and teachers, in particular, are very apt to observe that each school year's intake seems to have its own inherent characteristics.

There are also a number of ways by which the general characteristics of each animal-type can be refined to give a detailed character assessment of each individual. For just as anyone familiar with western astrology will know that the hour of birth reveals the 'ascendant' of the horoscope, the Chinese consider that the time at which person was born has an important bearing on future career and happiness. Other aspects which help to paint a more accurate picture of personality and fate are given by the month or season of birth: and the animal-types associated with each month may either strengthen or weaken the characteristics of the year-type. Thus, someone born in a Rat year would have his Rat characteristics emphasized if born in a Rat month, but toned down if born in the Horse month – the Rat's opposite sign.

The Chinese calendar is regulated by the phases of the Moon, and is therefore extremely complicated; but you will be able to get a good idea of which animal is associated with your particular birth month from the table on page 12.

Compatibility between animal types

Once you are familiar with your own animal sign, you will no doubt want to know the signs of others close to you, and then to establish the nature and extent of your compatibility.

There is a simple way to do this. If the names of the twelve animals are placed in order (Rat, Ox, Tiger, Hare, Dragon, Snake, Horse, Sheep, Monkey, Rooster, Dog, Pig) at the twelve positions of the hours of a clock-face, with your own birth-year animal at the twelve o'clock position, then the most compatible signs will be at the four o'clock and eight o'clock positions, compatible signs at two and ten o'clock, poor compatibility at three and nine o'clock, and adversity shown at the six o'clock position.

The Twelve Chinese Months and their Associated Animals

First month   approximating to February: *the Tiger*

Second month   approximating to March: *the Hare*
(The Hare month includes the Spring Equinox)

Third month   approximating to April: *the Dragon*

Fourth month   approximating to May: *the Snake*

Fifth month   approximating to June: *the Horse*
(The Horse month includes the Summer Solstice)

Sixth month   approximating to July: *the Sheep*

Seventh month   approximating to August: *the Monkey*

Eighth month   approximating to September: *the Rooster*
(The Rooster month includes the Autumn Equinox)

Ninth month   approximating to October: *the Dog*

Tenth month   approximating to November: *the Pig*

Eleventh month approximating to December: *the Rat*
(The Rat month includes the Winter Solstice)

Twelfth month   approximating to January: *the Ox*

Broadly-speaking, the most compatible signs fall into four groups of three: the Rat, Dragon, and Monkey; the Ox, Snake, and Rooster; the Tiger, Dog and Horse; and the Pig, Hare and Sheep. More detailed remarks on your relationships with other people, whether in business, within the family, in friendship or in romance, can be found on pages 25-28.

But to make a more specific comparison of two personalities, it is also important to take into account the interaction of the Five Elements.

The Five Elements

The Chinese sages of old taught that the Universe is kept in order by Five Elements – Wood, Fire, Earth, Metal and Water – and that one gives rise to the next in regular succession, or as the Chinese say: 'Wood burns, producing Fire; Fire leaves ash – or Earth – from which Metal is mined; Metal melts, like Water; and Water feeds growing Wood'; after which the whole cycle begins again.

Similarly, the order of the Five Elements can be likened to the progress of the year as it passes through five 'seasons', each associated with one of the elements. Spring, season of growth and creation, belongs to Wood; the hot season is governed by

Fire; the middle of the year, by the Earth element; the harvest, when ploughs cut into the Earth, by Metal; and finally, the cold, wet season, by Water.

In the Chinese calendar, years are counted in pairs according to the elements. Thus 1984 and 1985 were ruled by the Wood element, 1986 and 1987 by the Fire element, and so on. In this way, each year has both an animal name and an element; so that someone born in a particular year can be described not only as a particular animal type but also by the relevant element. This makes it possible to outline character assessments in greater detail: and just how the five elements influence your own particular animal sign is explained more fully on pages 19-20.

Compatibility between the element types

The usual order of the Five Elements is the 'generative' order, in which each element 'generates' the next in the series: and as a general rule, it can be said that two people will be compatible if their influencing elements stand in the generative order – a Wood-type and a Water-type, for instance. But there is also a 'destructive' order (Wood – Earth – Water – Fire – Metal), in which each successive element overpowers the other, and such combinations are usually found to be less fortunate. (Wood is said to absorb the goodness from Earth; Earth sullies Water; Water quenches Fire; Fire melts Metal; and Metal chops down Wood.)

From these two orders, it is easy to imagine how one element type may either help or hinder another. Positively, a Wood-type may provide the Fire person with resources; the Fire-type may stimulate the obstinate Earth; Earth may give stability to the rash Metal-type; Metal may give active support to the dreaming Water personality; and Water may provide the knowledge from which the Wood-type is able to create.

Conversely, the Wood-type may will be a drain on the Earth's reserves, perhaps of patience or even materially; an Earth-type could cause damage to Water's reputation; Water may quench the Fire-type's enthusiasm; Fire would be a very formidable opponent for the normally assertive Metal-type, who in turn might harrass Wood.

But what of the future, whatever your animal-type? Chinese astrologers maintain that the success or failure of plans can be foreseen by charting the progress of the Five Elements – whether they are dominant, recessive, waxing or waning: and by comparing the pattern of the Elements of a particular day with those of your own birth-date, Chinese astrologers are able to advise whether the day is likely to prove favourable or otherwise.

Now, with the help of this guide, you will be able to chart your own daily horoscope aspect from the step-by-step instructions given on pages 33–37.

Some people may claim that they do not wish to know what the future holds in store for them. But if there is danger ahead, is it not better to be forewarned? And if there is happiness, will it not give encouragement? Often we are faced with crises and decisions. By perusing your daily horoscope aspect, and taking into consideration the prevailing fortunate elements, problems and dilemmas can often be untangled, and the right direction made clearer.

It is my sincere hope that the knowledge and advice gathered for you from the many friends I have met during my travels to the temples and monasteries throughout China and the Far East will bring you a deeper insight and understanding of your true self, and your relationship with the world about you.

Derek Walters

丁酉神將臧文公

The
ROOSTER
Personality

*C*uriously enough, in China, the 'Hour of the Rooster' is sunset, not sunrise; and just as odd is the fact than in Chinese astrology, the male Rooster is regarded as a feminine sign. Perhaps these two paradoxes explain the complex personality of those born under its sign, who usually display both 'masculine' assertiveness and softer 'feminine' interests in life.

[17]

The Rooster has great self-pride, both in possessions and achievements, seeking recognition and acclaim, relentlessly pursuing whatever end is thought will achieve this. Some will regard wealth as the sign of success; others, fame: but some may regard a model home-life to be the ideal achievement. Thus, for the Rooster, life becomes a never-ending quest for perfection.

Abrasive and sometimes bordering on the aggressive, the Rooster frequently alienates people who interpret frankness as rudeness, and style as vanity, since shrewd business sense does not prevent the Rooster from making extravagant gestures when the timing is seen as appropriate.

Born in the Year of the Rooster

Donald Malcolm Campbell, Erroll Flynn, W. H. Smith,
Hermione Gingold, Lady Hamilton, Peter Ustinov

How the Five Elements affect the
ROOSTER *Personality*

The WOOD-Rooster
13 Feb 1945-1 Feb 1946

The element Wood adds creative talent to someone who already has great inventiveness and flair. Such a combination produces people with great artistic ability, and determination to excel in any field. They can be very exacting and make heavy demands on their colleagues and friends, however. In love, they are both passionate and romantic. Their ideal companion in life would be someone with the calming influence of the element Water in the birth-year sign.

The FIRE-Rooster
31 Jan 1957-17 Feb 1958

Certain traits in the Rooster's character portrait – excitability, competitiveness and flair – are all intensified by the element Fire. This produces an extrovert, fashion-conscious and popular personality who could succeed in the public eye. Personal life, however, tends to run less smoothly. Marriages are not always successful, and ideally the Fire-Rooster should choose someone born in an Earth year for security and peace of mind.

The EARTH-Rooster
22 Jan 1909-9 Feb 1910,   17 Feb 1969-5 Feb 1970

The Earth-Rooster is one of the more soundly practical of the five Rooster-types. A good organizer, careful with finances, and with a sense of style, this type of personality will be admired and respected. In love, the Earth-Rooster is fondly caring. A good marriage partner could be someone born in a Fire, Earth, or (for a woman Earth-Rooster) Metal year.

The METAL-Rooster
8 Feb 1921-27 Jan 1922,   5 Feb 1981-24 Jan 1982

Metal heightens the Rooster's competitiveness. This produces a character well able to deal with complex financial situations. In romantic affairs, the Metal-Rooster alternates between being aloof and demanding. The ideal life-companion would be under the influence of either the Earth or Water element.

The WATER-Rooster
26 Jan 1933-13 Feb 1934,   23 Jan 1993-9 Feb 1994

The gentler Rooster-types are those born in years ruled by the Water element, which softens the Rooster's more aggressive characteristics, and enhances a love for art and music. The Water-Rooster is warm and understanding, but dominant. Ideal companions would be born in a Metal or (for a male Water-Rooster) Earth year.

How the *ROOSTER*

fares in each animal year

In the Year of the *RAT*, *19 Feb 1996–6 Feb 1997*

This will be an adverse year for the Rooster. The Rat gnaws away at reserves, and the punctilious Rooster will not enjoy having to break into carefully saved funds. During this difficult period, it is advisable to take the greatest care in entering partnerships of either a business or romantic nature.

In the Year of the *OX*, *7 Feb 1997–27 Jan 1998*

After a particularly bad patch last year, the smooth running of the Ox Year is understandably welcome. The Rooster's natural flair for showmanship will find plenty of opportunities, and opinions are going to be sought after. There are strong indications of travel or promotion, if not both. Altogether, it will be a very fortunate year.

In the Year of the *TIGER*, *28 Jan 1998–15 Feb 1999*

This is a middling year for those born in the Year of the Rooster, neither harmonising nor clashing with the Tiger. The time is ideal for planning new ventures, whether in business or romance, if long-term affairs are sought. Opportunities abound.

In the Year of the *HARE*, *16 Feb 1999–4 Feb 2000*

There have been better times for those born in the Year of the Rooster. A general feeling of frustration arises due to the fact that finances and opportunities are never available at the same time. Fortunately, this is only a passing phase. Patience and caution are both advised.

In the Year of the *DRAGON*, *17 Feb 1988–5 Feb 1989*

This will be a very creative and constructive year for the Rooster, coming as a great improvement over the previous one. The influence of the Dragon adds stimulus, and there will be a general feeling that an onerous burden has been lifted. Personal relationships thrive.

In the Year of the *SNAKE*, *6 Feb 1989–26 Jan 1990*

For those born in the Year of the Rooster, this will prove to be an exceptionally successful year. Normally outgoing and forthright, the Rooster may decide to adopt many of the methods used by the Snake – discretion, tact, confidentiality – to make a considerable advance. Romantic affairs are highlighted. Finances are more secure.

In the Year of the *HORSE*, *27 Jan 1990–14 Feb 1991*

This is a mixed year for those born in the Year of the Rooster. Family life will be uppermost with more than its usual share of events, some bringing happiness; others, anxieties. Romance goes through a difficult phase. On the other hand, the year promises well for those involved in legal affairs.

In the Year of the *SHEEP*, *15 Feb 1991–3 Feb 1992*

This year is full of pleasant surprises for, although the Sheep Year is generally regarded as a mild, meditative period – quite the reverse of what the flamboyant Rooster usually enjoys – a broadening spectrum of activities will bring the Rooster into contact with many new friends with a variety of unusual interests.

In the Year of the *MONKEY*, *4 Feb 1992–22 Jan 1993*

The Rooster is the complementary sign to the Monkey, and many of the better aspects of the year rule in the Rooster's favour. Career ambitions are realised, and business expands satisfactorily. But though personal relationships flourish, this is not a good period for matters connected with the home.

In the Year of the *ROOSTER*, *23 Jan 1993–9 Feb 1994*

In every respect, apart from romance, this is an excellent year. Career activities move forward, and home life is both secure and rewarding. While the year may not be the best one for putting new ideas into practice, however, all goes superbly for well-established projects.

In the Year of the *DOG*, *10 Feb 1994–30 Jan 1995*

The Rooster must regard this as a time of challenge, otherwise continuous obstacles may be altogether disheartening. It is also wise to keep within the limits of the law, as minor legal wrangles appear. Avoid mixing romance with business. Both are favourably aspected but at different sides of the chart.

In the Year of the *PIG*, *31 Jan 1995–18 Feb 1996*

There is a marked improvement in general conditions this year, after a long, dull period. Family relationships are better, with some old disputes reconciled. Social events figure prominently, but it is a pity that many former, worthwhile activities are neglected.

ROOSTER Relationships

Find out how you relate to each
of the twelve animal signs, with specific reference
to interaction within the family, in business
and in romance. The tables on pages 46-48
provide a guide to each animal year.

with the Rat The Rooster will probably want more excitement in romance than the Rat will provide. In business, too, there may be many differences of opinion. The Rat-child will show independence to the parental Rooster.

with the Ox This relationship should prove lasting, even when romance disappears, forming what might be called a 'sensible arrangement'. Business prospects are very good; and the parental Rooster will greatly appreciate the Ox-child's steadiness and reliability.

with the Tiger There are too many conflicts of interest to make this a conventional relationship. Romance is tempestuous; business, uncomfortable. The Tiger-child should be nurtured carefully by the Rooster-parent. Great potential may otherwise go to waste.

with the Hare Initial physical attraction may not mean a permanent relationship. In business, meanwhile, each may resent the other's methods. The Hare-child may seem lazy and careless to the Rooster-parent.

with the Dragon These two exotic characters strike a respondent note romantically. In business, too, they are likely to respect each other's talents. The Dragon-child will never cease to mystify the parental Rooster.

with the Snake According to Chinese folk-lore, this relationship does not work in marriage. But in business, such partnerships are likely to do very well. The Snake-child will also bring praise to the Rooster-parent.

with the Horse Rooster and Horse have little in common, and a relationship, either in love or business, may therefore prove difficult to cement. The Horse-child is also likely to make his or her own way in life, independently of the Rooster-parent.

with the Sheep There is a great deal of love here, and it should be carefully nurtured. In business, the Sheep should also prove a worthy, hard-working partner for the Rooster. A Sheep-child will be very loyal and affectionate to the parental Rooster.

with the Monkey This is a curious but intriguing partnership, both in love and business, providing a few stormy moments, but generally a highly productive relationship. The Monkey-child should be handled with care by the Rooster-parent, or a brilliant career may be shattered.

with another Rooster Two Roosters can lead to confrontations, and each must afford the other a good deal of independence for a harmonious relationship in either love or business. The Rooster-parent should take care not to let the Rooster-child go his or her own way too early.

with the Dog Romantically, there could be unhappiness, unless the Rooster keeps career separate from home. In business, the Dog may shirk responsibility. The Dog-child will, however, always be loyal to the Rooster-parent.

with the Pig Both home and career are well-matched in this partnership, where each understands the other's point-of-view. The Pig-child will also be a great comfort to a Rooster-parent in later life.

How the Hour of Birth affects
the Fate of
the ROOSTER Personality

Born during the *RAT* hour (11pm-1am)

Gifted, as you are, with many talents and a spirit of competition, your success will be due to personal abilities, but care must be taken not to risk everything in trying to achieve unrealistic goals. Take particular care in the choice of a life companion.

Born during the *OX* hour (1am-3am)

Flair and talent are combined with tenacity and persistence, leading to success in your chosen field. No goal will be too distant for you. Do not speculate, however, and avoid romantic ideals.

Born during the *TIGER* hour (3am-5am)

Use your latent abilities to their best advantage. In business, distribution and commerce fare better than manufacture; and travelling will bring wealth. Marriage will give you security and personal contentment, but family ties are otherwise not strong.

Born during the *HARE* hour (5am-7am)

Health may bring problems; and the romantic side of marriage may disappoint, but your children will be a source of joy and contentment. Personal reward is likely to come through social service.

Born during the *DRAGON* hour (7am-9am)

The signs indicate interests in investment and speculation. Use your personal knowledge and instinct; but as finances fluctuate, never risk everything. In romance, personal happiness is assured.

Born during the *SNAKE* hour (9am-11am)

There are excellent prospects for combining intelligence with an eye for current trends, and good aspects for the conversationalist, journalist and dramatist but less favourable signs for the practical worker or artist. Romantic life may disappoint.

Born during the *HORSE* hour (11am-1pm)

Wealth may be attained through a fortunate marriage, bringing property and possessions, but possibly at the expense of personal happiness. Land, houses, and foreign travel are all promised. Do not neglect your health.

Born during the *SHEEP* hour (1pm-3pm)

Your heart will often rule your head, but fame and fortune take second place to personal happiness. There will be a contented marriage, and children who bring joy to their parents are the rewards to be reaped.

Born during the *MONKEY* hour (3pm-5pm)

There are excellent prospects here, with an agile and lively mind, and an ability to see things through. Less favourable aspects exist, however, for romance, marriage and the family.

Born during the *ROOSTER* hour (5pm-7pm)

The positive aspects of the basic Rooster personality – determination, flair, and judgement – are all emphasized. High standards will lead to personal achievement; and favourable aspects exist for wealth and property. Prospects regarding romance and marriage are not so reassuring, however; and health may pose problems.

Born during the *DOG* hour (7pm-9pm)

Favourable aspects are foreseen for marriage, possessions, property, and foreign travel, but you need a supportive partner. After some disappointments, the true life companion will be found.

Born during the *PIG* hour (9pm-11pm)

A successful marriage, a happy family, and rewarding children are important objectives to you in life, and resources will be needed to secure these ends. But commerce and manufacturing are not highly rated, and moderate financial independence only may be achieved.

Casting a daily horoscope

*T*he Chinese have always been very down-to-earth in their approach to astrology; and while they find it fascinating to learn about their inner selves and to know how they stand in their personal relationships, they are much more likely to expect an astrologer to give them sound, practical advice on everyday matters.

Chinese astrology is certainly able to do much more than reveal the complexities of your personality. Indeed, by drafting an individual daily horoscope forecast, it is possible to discover which days will be best suited for business and social life, when you may need to take special care, when you would do best to stay at home rather than embarking on a long journey, or when you are likely to meet with particularly good fortune.

On the pages that follow, you will find the basic method for casting your own personal daily horoscope, carefully set out, step by step. No mathematical prowess is needed, just an ability to add and subtract a few simple figures. These straightforward calculations will enable you to find the cyclic number for your date of birth, and any other date this century. (These numbers are an exact match with those published in the official Chinese astrological calendar, the oldest in the world, and still in continuous use after more than three thousand years.) These two numbers are then compared to find the *aspect number* which reveals the daily forecast given in the final section.

How to Calculate Your Own Personal Daily Horoscope Aspect

(Note: The Chinese day begins at 11pm: so if you were born between 11pm and midnight, base your calculations on the day following your birthdate.)

Take a piece of paper, preferably lined, and write the letters A to K in a column down the left-hand side.

Finding the cyclic number for your date of birth

[A] At A on your sheet of paper, write the *date* of the month of your birth: i.e. if you were born on 12th April, write 12.

[B] Using Table I on page 45, find the code number for your month of birth and write this at B.

[C] Using Table II on page 45, find the code number for your year of birth and write this at C.

[D] If you were born on or after February 29th during a leap-year, put 1 at D. Otherwise put O. (A leap year is one which is divisible by 4; 1988 is therefore a leap year).

[E] Add the figures at A, B, C and D.
If the result is 121 or more, subtract 120; if the figure is between 61 and 120, subtract 60. Write the result at E.

This is the *cyclic number for your birthdate*.

Finding the cyclic number for any date this century

You will need to follow the same procedure outlined in steps A to D to find the cyclic number for any required day this century.

[F] Write the *date* of the month of the required date at F.

[G] Write the *monthly* code number for the required month at G.

[H] Write the *yearly* code number for the required year at H.

[I] Write the figure 1 at I, if a leap-year adjustment is required. Otherwise put O.

[J] Add the figures at F, G, H and I.

If the total is 121 or more, subtract 120; if the figure is between 61 and 120, subtract 60. Write the result at J.

This is the *cyclic number for the required date*.

Finding your personal daily aspect number

First note whether the cyclic number for your birthdate (E) is *yang* (an *odd* number) or *yin* (an even number.)

(i) If the cyclic number for your birthdate (E) is *yang* (odd):
> from the cyclic number for the required date (J)
> SUBTRACT
> the cyclic number for the birthdate (E).
> (Note. If J is less then E, first add 60.)
> Write your result at K.

(ii) If the cyclic number for your birthdate (E) is *yin* (even):
> from the cyclic number for the birthdate (E)
> SUBTRACT
> the cyclic number for the required date (J).
> (Note. If E is less than J, first add 60.)
> Write your result at K.

The figure at K is your *Personal Daily Aspect Number*. Now turn to pages 38–44 to find your own personal forecast for the required date.

Your Personal Daily Horoscope Aspects

[0] *See aspect 60.*

[1] The Rooster will find this to be a rewarding day, with success in many fields. Those involved in creative or artistic ventures are bound to succeed. Social life is highlighted, too.

[2] The Rooster will find this an ideal day for short journeys. Conditions are less favourable for routine matters, however.

[3] You will have some exciting ideas regarding home improvements which you should follow up. Business runs well; and today is much better for routine work.

[4] You may need to take advice regarding someone in your family, but leave any decision for a while. Try not to be persuaded against your better judgement, and weigh up with care the helpful suggestions which you receive.

[5] This is an ideal day for most matters, especially if travelling is involved. However, in legal matters the position is less secure.

[6] Do not act too hastily regarding relationships. Your leisure plans go well. Take care when working with sharp implements.

[7] The Rooster's prospects for today continue to improve though there may be a few obstacles regarding commercial transactions. There is a chance of promotion and the prospect of a better financial position for those able to make time available for study.

[8] While the day passes peacably enough, you will not get through

everything you wanted to do. However, you can still proceed with confidence.

[9] There are obstacles ahead, so be prepared to put a lot of effort into your activities today. Take advice on any matters concerning children. A chance meeting leads to friendship.

[10] You may feel like making changes to your plans. Act on any ideas you have, and use your contacts.

[11] This is a particularly demanding, but nevertheless highly successful day. Keep on sure ground, and stick to family matters.

[12] This is a good day for you to try to improve your image. Now that finances are more secure, there is a chance to buy something you have always wanted.

[13] Conditions are favourable for all matters to do with the home and personal life. Use your knowledge of present conditions to put your plans into action.

[14] There is an improved position today with respect to career prospects, but otherwise little change apart from an unexpected windfall. It is a good day for selling, and for anything concerning personal appearance.

[15] Exciting promises are off-set by disappointments today. Avoid dealing with legal matters.

[16] Take care when dealing with casual acquaintances. Do not involve them in your personal problems. Business and commercial activities fare successfully.

[17] For most activities it will be a particularly demanding, but nevertheless highly successful day. There may be problems in your personal life, however.

[18] There are highly favourable prospects today for matters involving land, and for all long-term projects which have been established for some time. Plan your journeys carefully.

[19] It would be advisable today not to get too involved in situations where the people are not known to you personally. Take advice if you are worried about your health.

[20] For the Rooster, this is generally a smooth-running day. No areas are particularly highlighted, but neither are there any dangerous pitfalls. The early evening will bring interesting news.

[21] While all signs are for the most part favourable, there will be greater expenditure than expected. However, you will achieve your objectives.

[22] This is a day when it is important to take care not to strain your resources, physical and financial. Keep away from personal confrontation, and avoid unnecessary travel.

[23] It will be an excellent day for your personal ambitions, and all practical matters will be successful.

[24] Although this is not an outstanding day in your diary, there is a pleasant surprise in store for you.

[25] The Rooster is unlikely to get through today without argument and some wrangling, and will have to work hard to succeed.

[26] Although today's achievements will be below par, you will find

you have a renewed vitality and gain greater inner confidence.

[27] Today will be an exhausting one, but it also brings great benefits. Expect greater demands on you at work, leading to possible promotion. Dealings with employees or subordinates will progress very well.

[28] Conditions are not favourable at the moment for getting things done, even though you may feel in a creative mood. It is a better day for planning than achieving. Do not take financial risks at all today.

[29] Matters remain fairly stable, with little difference in conditions generally at home or at work. This enables you to get on with the task in hand without distractions.

[30] The Rooster will find this a good day for team activities; but social events are best when they are with colleagues rather than family. Expect some setbacks, and put down losses to experience.

[31] This will be an enjoyable day, but be prepared for unexpected calls on your finances. You are likely to be asked to join in some socializing to celebrate a friend's success.

[32] Matters may go smoothly at work, but there may be upsets at home. Be prepared for a frustrating time, and keep your head.

[33] This is a favourable day for personal achievement; and matters generally turn out well, particularly with regards to romance and social life. Some unexpected financial reward is also foreseen.

[34] It is a good day for romance and leisure. In solid, practical matters, however, conditions are unfavourable. Avoid getting anxious over temporary setbacks, and try not to take matters too seriously.

[35] Anything to do with the house or family is highlighted for the Rooster today. It is an excellent time for buying or selling land, or for signing contracts to do with the home or its furnishings. There is good news regarding health matters, either for yourself or your family.

[36] It will be an above-average day, which sees you feeling physical improvement. There are ideal conditions at home.

[37] This is not one of your best days. Be careful in your dealings with others, whether on a romantic, social or business level; and try to avoid situations which are going to demand your best responses.

[38] Although practically you may not achieve much today, you will have laid the groundwork for future expansion. On the face of it, there will be little to show, but you will be inwardly satisfied by today's steady progress.

[39] Conditions are generally unchanged, which will enable you to go ahead as planned.

[40] The Rooster will find conditions favourable for dealing with contracts and the signing of documents. There are particularly encouraging results in any matters involving children.

[41] Although this is generally a favourable day for all kinds of activity, expect some set-backs. Your expenditure will be greater than anticipated too.

[42] Try to take things easily today. Hasty actions may lead to accidents. There are highly favourable prospects for your personal correspondence.

[43] This is an extremely favourable day for commercial transactions

generally, and for anything involving construction, artistic activities, or travel at home or abroad.

[44] This is a good, steady day when you will have confidence in both your business and your personal relationships. Matters generally remain fairly stable. This enables you to get on with the task in hand without distractions.

[45] There are highly favourable prospects today for the Rooster. Use present trends to their best advantage. You will be best working away from home, but do not waste time in unnecessary travelling.

[46] It is unfortunately not a good day for dealings with colleagues, family, or circumstances where you have to assert yourself.

[47] You should take advice today regarding commercial transactions generally. In the end, the results will be well worth it.

[48] Renewed strength and confidence will help you to obtain your objectives today. There could also be a chance of promotion.

[49] Conditions remain generally unchanged, and all the minor irritations are still with you. Keep in the background, and try to learn from other people's mistakes.

[50] It will be an ideal day for matters relating to friends, while romance is also a possibility. Business ticks over; but don't organize anything too demanding for today.

[51] You may find yourself involved in a lot of strenuous leisure activity today, as the accent appears to be on enjoyment. Expect some set-backs regarding the signing of documents.

[52] It is a day when things may seem to get on top of you. Try not

to get involved in open-ended situations. You will just have to tolerate people's awkwardness a little longer. Stick to the tried and trusted.

[53] This is a good day for travel plans and matters relating to friends. A financial bonus is also a possibility.

[54] The signs are generally harmonious and peaceful. Plan ahead carefully, and keep objectives short-term.

[55] Conditions are very favourable today for home and family matters. Career prospects are also highlighted. But avoid travel that has not been carefully planned.

[56] There are very good prospects today. Renewed vigour and self-confidence will enable you to succeed in both business and personal matters. Take further advice if you are thinking of moving house.

[57] It will be a highly successful day, but you will be glad when it is all over.

[58] Proceed with confidence in respect of creative planning, rather than constructive, practical matters. Avoid gambling, or anything involving financial risk today.

[59] Use the present stable conditions to their best advantage. This is a good time for looking over any contracts involving land, or for any business ideas involving younger people.

[60][0] Proceed with confidence. Prospects for health, travel, home-life, business and romance are excellent.

TABLE I
Code number for the month

Month	Jan	Feb	Mar	April	May	June	July	Aug	Sept	Oct	Nov	Dec
Code	0	31	59	30	0	31	1	32	3	35	4	34

TABLE II
Code number for the year

Year	1901	1902	1903	1904	1905	1906	1907	1908	1909	1910	1911	1912
Code	15	20	25	30	36	41	46	51	57	2	7	12

Year	1913	1914	1915	1916	1917	1918	1919	1920	1921	1922	1923	1924
Code	18	23	28	33	39	44	49	54	0	5	10	15

Year	1925	1926	1927	1928	1929	1930	1931	1932	1933	1934	1935	1936
Code	21	26	31	36	42	47	52	57	3	8	13	18

Year	1937	1938	1939	1940	1941	1942	1943	1944	1945	1946	1947	1948
Code	24	29	34	39	45	50	55	0	6	11	16	21

Year	1949	1950	1951	1952	1953	1954	1955	1956	1957	1958	1959	1960
Code	27	32	37	42	48	53	58	3	9	14	19	24

Year	1961	1962	1963	1964	1965	1966	1967	1968	1969	1970	1971	1972
Code	30	35	40	45	51	56	1	6	12	17	22	27

Year	1973	1974	1975	1976	1977	1978	1979	1980	1981	1982	1983	1984
Code	33	38	43	48	54	59	4	9	15	20	25	30

Year	1985	1986	1987	1988	1989	1990	1991	1992	1993	1994	1995	1996
Code	36	41	46	51	57	2	7	12	18	23	28	33

Year	1997	1998	1999	2000
Code	39	44	49	54

The Chinese Calendar

19 Feb 1901 – 7 Feb 1902
Metal-Ox

8 Feb 1902 – 28 Jan 1903
Water-Tiger

29 Jan 1903 – 15 Feb 1904
Water-Hare

16 Feb 1904 – 3 Feb 1905
Wood-Dragon

4 Feb 1905 – 24 Jan 1906
Wood-Snake

25 Jan 1906 – 12 Feb 1907
Fire-Horse

13 Feb 1907 – 1 Feb 1908
Fire-Sheep

2 Feb 1908 – 21 Jan 1909
Earth-Monkey

22 Jan 1909 – 9 Feb 1910
Earth-Rooster

10 Feb 1910 – 29 Jan 1911
Metal-Dog

30 Jan 1911 – 17 Feb 1912
Metal-Pig

18 Feb 1912 – 5 Feb 1913
Water-Rat

6 Feb 1913 – 25 Jan 1914
Water-Ox

26 Jan 1914 – 13 Feb 1915
Wood-Tiger

14 Feb 1915 – 2 Feb 1916
Wood-Hare

3 Feb 1916 – 22 Jan 1917
Fire-Dragon

23 Jan 1917 – 10 Feb 1918
Fire-Snake

11 Feb 1918 – 31 Jan 1919
Earth-Horse

1 Feb 1919 – 19 Feb 1920
Earth-Sheep

20 Feb 1920 – 7 Feb 1921
Metal-Monkey

8 Feb 1921 – 27 Jan 1922
Metal-Rooster

28 Jan 1922 – 15 Feb 1923
Water-Dog

16 Feb 1923 – 4 Feb 1924
Water-Pig

5 Feb 1924 – 24 Jan 1925
Wood-Rat

25 Jan 1925 – 12 Feb 1926
Wood-Ox

13 Feb 1926 – 1 Feb 1927
Fire-Tiger

2 Feb 1927 – 22 Jan 1928
Fire-Hare

23 Jan 1928 – 9 Feb 1929
Earth-Dragon

8 Feb 1940 – 26 Jan 1941
Metal-Dragon

27 Jan 1952 – 13 Feb 1953
Water-Dragon

10 Feb 1929 – 29 Jan 1930
Earth-Snake

27 Jan 1941 – 14 Feb 1942
Metal-Snake

14 Feb 1953 – 2 Feb 1954
Water-Snake

30 Jan 1930 – 16 Feb 1931
Metal-Horse

15 Feb 1942 – 4 Feb 1943
Water-Horse

3 Feb 1954 – 23 Jan 1955
Wood-Horse

17 Feb 1931 – 5 Feb 1932
Metal-Sheep

5 Feb 1943 – 24 Jan 1944
Water-Sheep

24 Jan 1955 – 11 Feb 1956
Wood-Sheep

6 Feb 1932 – 25 Jan 1933
Water-Monkey

25 Jan 1944 – 12 Feb 1945
Wood-Monkey

12 Feb 1956 – 30 Jan 1957
Fire-Monkey

26 Jan 1933 – 13 Feb 1934
Water-Rooster

13 Feb 1945 – 1 Feb 1946
Wood-Rooster

31 Jan 1957 – 17 Feb 1958
Fire-Rooster

14 Feb 1934 – 3 Feb 1935
Wood-Dog

2 Feb 1946 – 21 Jan 1947
Fire-Dog

18 Feb 1958 – 7 Feb 1959
Earth-Dog

4 Feb 1935 – 23 Jan 1936
Wood-Pig

22 Jan 1947 – 9 Feb 1948
Fire-Pig

8 Feb 1959 – 27 Jan 1960
Earth-Pig

24 Jan 1936 – 10 Feb 1937
Fire-Rat

10 Feb 1948 – 28 Jan 1949
Earth-Rat

28 Jan 1960 – 14 Feb 1961
Metal-Rat

11 Feb 1937 – 30 Jan 1938
Fire-Ox

29 Jan 1949 – 16 Feb 1950
Earth-Ox

15 Feb 1961 – 4 Feb 1962
Metal-Ox

31 Jan 1938 – 18 Feb 1939
Earth-Tiger

17 Feb 1950 – 5 Feb 1951
Metal-Tiger

5 Feb 1962 – 24 Jan 1963
Water-Tiger

19 Feb 1939 – 7 Feb 1940
Earth-Hare

6 Feb 1951 – 26 Jan 1952
Metal-Hare

25 Jan 1963 – 12 Feb 1964
Water-Hare

13 Feb 1964 – 1 Feb 1965
Wood-Dragon

2 Feb 1965 – 20 Jan 1966
Wood-Snake

21 Jan 1966 – 8 Feb 1967
Fire-Horse

9 Feb 1967 – 29 Jan 1968
Fire-Sheep

30 Jan 1968 – 16 Feb 1969
Earth-Monkey

17 Feb 1969 – 5 Feb 1970
Earth-Rooster

6 Feb 1970 – 26 Jan 1971
Metal-Dog

27 Jan 1971 – 14 Feb 1972
Metal-Pig

15 Feb 1972 – 2 Feb 1973
Water-Rat

3 Feb 1973 – 22 Jan 1974
Water-Ox

23 Jan 1974 – 10 Feb 1975
Wood-Tiger

11 Feb 1975 – 30 Jan 1976
Wood-Hare

31 Jan 1976 – 17 Feb 1977
Fire-Dragon

18 Feb 1977 – 6 Feb 1978
Fire-Snake

7 Feb 1978 – 27 Jan 1979
Earth-Horse

28 Jan 1979 – 15 Feb 1980
Earth-Sheep

16 Feb 1980 – 4 Feb 1981
Metal-Monkey

5 Feb 1981 – 24 Jan 1982
Metal-Rooster

25 Jan 1982 – 12 Feb 1983
Water-Dog

13 Feb 1983 – 1 Feb 1984
Water-Pig

2 Feb 1984 – 19 Feb 1985
Wood-Rat

20 Feb 1985 – 8 Feb 1986
Wood-Ox

9 Feb 1986 – 28 Jan 1987
Fire-Tiger

29 Jan 1987 – 16 Feb 1988
Fire-Hare

17 Feb 1988 – 5 Feb 1989
Earth-Dragon

6 Feb 1989 – 26 Jan 1990
Earth-Snake

27 Jan 1990 – 14 Feb 1991
Metal-Horse

15 Feb 1991 – 3 Feb 1992
Metal-Sheep

4 Feb 1992 – 22 Jan 1993
Water-Monkey

23 Jan 1993 – 9 Feb 1994
Water-Rooster

10 Feb 1994 – 30 Jan 1995
Wood-Dog

31 Jan 1995 – 18 Feb 1996
Wood-Pig

19 Feb 1996 – 6 Feb 1997
Fire-Rat

7 Feb 1997 – 27 Jan 1998
Fire-Ox

28 Jan 1998 – 15 Feb 1999
Earth-Tiger

16 Feb 1999 – 4 Feb 2000
Earth-Hare